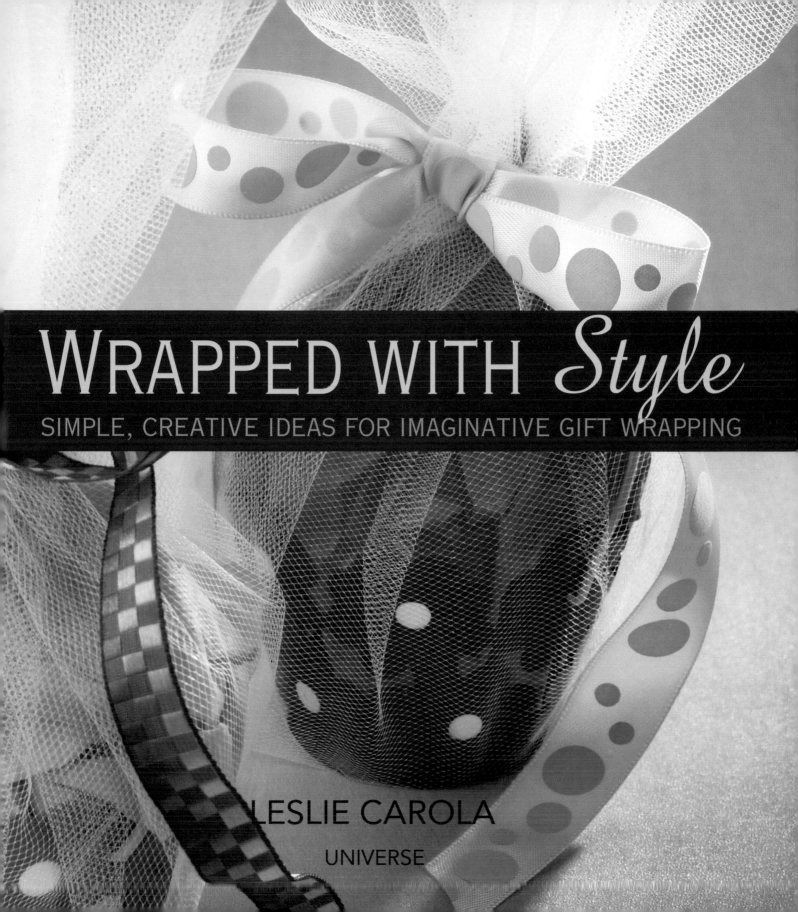

# WRAPPED WITH *Style*

## SIMPLE, CREATIVE IDEAS FOR IMAGINATIVE GIFT WRAPPING

LESLIE CAROLA

UNIVERSE

Published by UNIVERSE PUBLISHING
A Division of Rizzoli International Publications, Inc.
300 Park Avenue South
New York, NY 10010
www.rizzoliusa.com

An Arena Books Associates Book

Book concept and development: Leslie Carola
Design: Elizabeth Johnsboen
Photographer: Jon Van Gorder, except for pages 52–53 and 61 by Steve Aja

Acknowledgments: Thank you to the contributors—individual designers, artists, and crafters—who have contributed projects:
Jackquelin Cutrone, floral designer; Jane Gibbons; Andrea Grossman and Mrs. Grossman's Paper Company (www.mrsgrossmans.com); Nathalie Métivier, Magenta (www.magentastyle.com); Kitty Okamura and Cassie Mimbu, pinestreet papery (www.papery.com); Judy Ritchie and Jamie Kilmartin (www.greatamericanstampstore.com); Susan Swan (www.susanswan.com); Janet Williams. And thank you to Jim Muschett, Melissa Payne, Candice Fehrman, and Debby Zindell.

Contributors are credited on each page. Projects without credit were created by Leslie Carola.

2009  2010  2011  2012 /
10 9 8 7 6 5 4 3 2 1

Printed in China

ISBN-13: 978-0-7893-9954-0

Library of Congress
Catalog Control Number:
2008933179

# CONTENTS

# INTRODUCTION

$\mathcal{M}$uch of the fun of wrapping stylish gifts is selecting the raw materials—paper or fabric; bag or box; ribbon, yarn, or fibers. The variety of materials available is amazing and inspiring. And while it is true that the thought is what counts, I think the wrapping can be as exciting as the gift itself. Gifts come alive, so to speak, when the wrapping celebrates both the occasion and the individuals. The presentation pleases even before the gift is revealed. There is poetry in seeing the rhythm, the play of one shape on another. A beautifully

pinestreet papery

wrapped package delights the eye, and teases the senses. In addition to standard wrapping paper, consider using pieces of wallpaper, colorful tissue paper, plain white shelf paper, brown paper, handmade papers of varying weights and textures, silk fabric, linen, and so on. And of course you can include small bags, baskets, and boxes as part of your gift-wrapping repertoire. Try decorating with unusual embellishments. The possibilities are many.

The purpose of *Wrapped with Style* is to flood your senses with ideas: design ideas, as well as playful and dramatic color ideas. We

Janet Williams

7

Susan Swan

have gathered creative, achievable, festive gift wrapping from individual crafters and gift wrappers from across the country. Good things come in all manner of packages. Many of the projects are simple, and many are elegant. Some are sophisticated, some are fun, a few are zany, and there is at least one outrageous project. Beautiful wrapping is treasured as a gift itself, transient though it may be, leading to the treasure within.

Paper and ribbon are such remarkable materials—each is colorful, sensual, and pliable. Who can resist a beautiful sheet of paper or a stunning ribbon? How many times have you reached out to stroke, pinch, ruffle, or straighten either one? We use paper more often than other materials when wrapping gifts because it is such a pleasure to work with. And the ribbons are works of art in themselves, adding color, texture, and dimension to a package. Take some time to think. Think of color, shape, and texture. Imagine what would be fun for you, then try it. The personal touch of a specially wrapped gift lets the recipient know how much he or she means to you. If you enjoy wrapping a gift the recipient will enjoy receiving the gift. Keep the occasion in mind. Feeling witty? Nostalgic? Sophisticated? Create something from your heart. Stretch your imagination, express your creativity. And have fun!

PLAYING
WITH COLOR

Gift wrapping is just as important as choosing the gift itself. And it can be just as much fun. A well-wrapped package is created with a good sense of design. Rules for good design are few, but some elements should be considered: who is the recipient and what is the occasion? How do you want the recipient to feel when opening the package? What message do you want to send? Your feelings about the recipient can help you create the most appropriate wrapping. Trust your own eye to tell you what "works." Color elicits a powerful emotional reaction in us, and it sets the tone. Generally, warm colors—yellow, orange, and red—generate excitement, while cool colors—blue and green—are soothing. Mix and match colors to your taste. The charming metal baskets, opposite, seen through white tulle, are ideal vehicles for small gifts tucked in colorful tissue paper.

etting the color combination of paper and ribbon just right can be daunting, but it is a satisfying process. Experiment with colors that you like to see together. Find hues and tints of colors in the

Paper/tag: Susan Swan

paper and ribbon to complement or accent. Step back and see the play of one color with another. The hand-sponged orange paper left, at rear, quietly accepts and *displays* the gold-bronze ribbon. The paper and ribbon share a harmonious palette. The green of the polka-dot ribbon, at front, contrasts with the paper, while the tag decoration cut from the wrapping paper provides a unifying link.

[Opposite, front] The narrow green ribbon adds contrast, while the orange polka dots anchor the palette. The generously sized cone adds shape and dimension to a small package.

[Opposite, rear] Extra-wide ribbon and an oversized bow create the central appeal of the package.

[Above] Gold-bronze flocked floral shapes parade in orderly rows on a turquoise paper. We focused attention on the paper pattern by wrapping the ribbon around the package at diagonal corners. The cool-blue paper is a powerful stage on which to present the warmth of the gold-toned ribbon.

[Opposite] A display of richly colored ribbons promotes festive ideas. We have come a long way from simple swirls of paper ribbons on our gifts. Here we have included beautiful lightweight organdy ribbon, thick embroidered satin ribbon, pastel woven ribbon, and printed ribbon in varying styles ranging from polka dots to ginghams, checks, and stripes.

[Above] Dramatic, imaginative Father's Day gift wrap offers simple solutions with an appropriate palette.

here are many tantalizing papers and ribbons available today. The colorful embroidered turquoise paper below, at rear, is particularly enticing. The turquoise color is restated in the embroidery and then mixed with deep blue, apple green, and silver threads.

Narrow silver cord winding through the bow echoes the silver threads in the paper. The tiny dot pattern of green on blue in the paper at front becomes a rich chorus with the tiny dot pattern of blue on green in the wired ribbon. Wired ribbon not only makes tying bows easy, it also helps them keep their shape on the package. Should the handsome bows get crushed, they are easily refreshed with a tweak.

[Opposite] The richly textured paper at rear needs no more than subtle ribbons. Reversed color patterns on the paper and ribbon at front create a balanced harmony.

[Above] Playing with cool and warm colors allows us to see the effect of color immediately. Here the colors in the paper change as the light and decorative elements change. Embellishments in warm and cool tones—a warm silk rose or a cool organdy ribbon with a quilled tag—are equally expressive.

A solid red paper lends itself to a variety of treatments. This cheerful multicolored checkered ribbon has a warm, rustic, handmade look to it. The rubber-stamped, hand-quilled gift tag adds a further homespun note to the gift. For stable, sculptural bows, use wired ribbon. The delightful gift, opposite, is ingenious. Several small gifts are lined up on clear acetate, wrapped as one, and separated by a green ribbon, knotted between each one to form a segmented snake with a poison-green head and orange forked tongue—a child's delight.

By making the gift part of the gift wrap you focus attention on the process and design of the wrapping. This is a project I couldn't resist—whimsical, summery sherbet-colored, ice-cream-cone-shaped candles (bought on a wintery Vermont day) are perfect embellishments for their own package. We wrapped a small cube box without its top in fuchsia tissue paper, tucking the paper over the top edge of the box and securing it with double-sided tape inside the box. Clean, flat corners can be made by cutting a diagonal line from the edge of the paper tucked inside the box to the corner and taping each side carefully. A simple bow is tied around the box with a two-sided satin ribbon—pistachio and raspberry, of course. We inserted the candles into a block of floral foam cut to fit the box, cradled the foam in violet tissue paper, and inserted the whole ensemble into the wrapped box.

The tags below and opposite are stamped with rubber stamps from Magenta. Below, the ink is coordinated with berry-stained paper and a darker purple satin ribbon. Opposite, a pink fabric flower on each of the three rows of pink-and-white ribbon accentuates the palette and design. A double pleat as seen at front—which can be horizontal or vertical—creates added interest. It serves as a pocket to hold a tag (see instructions on page 116). The tag is stamped in white ink on white cardstock, embossed with white embossing powder, and painted with watercolors. The embossed areas resist color.

[Opposite] A tumble of summery-colored ribbons reminds us of long, lazy days, refreshing fruit sherbets, and lovely hair ribbons. Packages wrapped in summertime style are carefree and colorful. [Above] A simple violet paper with tiny white dots is the perfect backdrop for a full twisted-loop bow of elegant, sheer, white organdy ribbon. The easy-to-make dark violet tag is embellished with a pearl-studded decoration.

A combination of red and gold sings of winter holiday celebrations. The wonderful red paper below showcases clean, large gold squares. Wide, gold, wired ribbon tied in a simple bow with graceful, long tails was a natural choice, as was the quilled gold snowflake ornament on a white disc. The ornament, part of the gift, also functions as the gift tag. Each recipient receives a different ornament so the gift giver knows exactly who is to receive each package. The color-coordinated holiday wreath of individually wrapped small gifts in combinations of red, white, and green papers, opposite, almost begs to be left intact for the season. The papers, the ribbons separating the sections, and the bows add to the merriment and good cheer. The clear acetate final covering keeps all of those gaily wrapped presents in view. This delightful package was made much like the imaginative snake package on page 21.

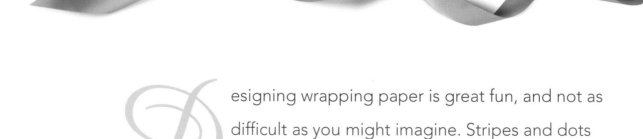

Designing wrapping paper is great fun, and not as difficult as you might imagine. Stripes and dots are easily created in Adobe Photoshop or other image-editing software. Once in Photoshop, paper colors can be changed to provide a limitless supply of your own designed wrapping paper. Or try creating papers by painting them. Inspiration for your paper designs can be found everywhere. Take a walk and observe the shapes, patterns, and colors around you. The bold black-and-white paper at left was painted, scanned, and color adjusted in Adobe Photoshop.

Susan Swan

Susan Swan

[Opposite] A simple palette can offer a bold statement, like this strong black-and-white paper and imaginative, coordinated tags. The larger "2" gift tag is an inventive collage.

[Above] These three papers engage us: the repetitive arrangement of uneven white circles on black paper is eye catching; the marbled blue and spattered red sheets are warm and pleasing.

# TYING IT UP

aper can be so irresistible. It begs to be touched, stroked, or patted. Ribbons elicit a very similar response in us. I often take a special ribbon from a gift to wind around my fingers and save for future use. And when I do, I am reminded of my mother and grandmother who did the same in quiet gestures. Sometimes my grandmother would tuck the wound ribbon in a delicate porcelain lidded dish sitting on a table at her side. As a child I would always peek inside the dish each time I visited her to see if she had forgotten to gather the wound ribbons. She never had. Ribbon styles are many: narrow or wide, thick or thin, textured or smooth, patterned or solid, wired or flat. Ways of using ribbons are also many: subtle or obvious, bow or none, multilooped or single, one ribbon or more. Ribbons layered or bedecked with dainty roses, opposite, extend the palette and add depth.

$\mathcal{T}$he kind of ribbon, the weight, the width, the color, and the way it is used on a package affects the look and feel of a wrapped gift. To tie or not to tie is often an appropriate question. The answer depends on the effect you want. We had fun wrapping ribbons around boxes that were covered with the same paper to show what a change of ribbon could do. Not a bow in sight! Denim blue paper can be dressed up or down for a refined or casual occasion. Creative ribbon choice and placement can make a plain package stunning.

Three different ribbon treatments create three looks on gifts wrapped with the same paper.

[Opposite] Puffy silver stars layered on red mesh offer interesting texture and a comfortable patriotic look, perfect for a Fourth of July celebration.

[Above, left] Fresh flowers are always appropriate. Here pretty red and blue flowers, also perfect for a Fourth of July celebration, are tucked easily under a wide white satin ribbon stretched across the corner of a gift wrapped in denim blue paper. The wide ribbon allows us to conceal the flower stems enclosed in a florist's vial.

[Above, right] A double row of khaki, white, and denim blue ribbon offers a casually refined look on a gift wrapped for a man.

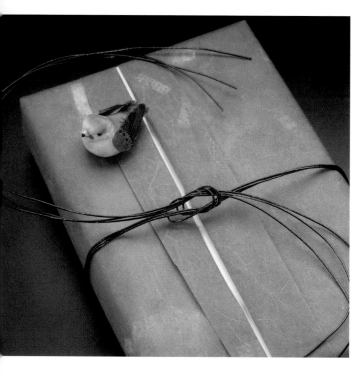

Although ribbons are not *essential* for a beautifully wrapped package, they are a festive addition, enhancing dimension and color. A traditional Japanese dyed and starched cord for wrapping— mizuhiki—provides an elegant finishing touch to a package. The starched cords have become popular embellishments for paper crafters and are now available in several colors and weights in craft stores. I sometimes wrap a gift with a narrow vertical fold opening at the front of the package, centered or off-center, revealing a contrasting strip of box beneath the paper. The soft moss green handmade paper for the package at left folds easily and lies flat. Several strands of bronze mizuhiki wrap around the box and tie in a simple knot with large swooping tails cradling a small bird sitting at top left.

pinestreet papery

[Above] Richly textured, ribbed orange ribbon tied in a lavish bow of soft loops and generous tails provides contrast against the flat, smooth box. Tucking a small butterfly into the folds of the bow adds a delicate finishing touch.

Susan Swan

pinestreet papery

[Opposite] A stunning orange flower cut from wrapping paper takes the place of a bow. A piece of netting and one button create texture and dimension at the center of the flower anchored to two patterned ribbons. The beige and rust ribbon is actually a strip of fabric with deliberately frayed edges. Various cords and fibers hold the flower in place on the brown-paper-wrapped package.

[Above] A glassy-eyed orange fish hides in the multilooped bow atop a fuschia-wrapped box. Active colors, such as the contrasting fuschia and orange, generate excitement.

The choices for a wrapping style are many: innovative or traditional, elegant or whimsical, sophisticated or simple; fill the surface, spotlight one feature, create a simple, quiet palette or a raucous melange of color. Brilliant red, soft, organdy ribbon with a delicate wired edge ties into a rich multilooped bow at the center of a classic wrapped gift box, opposite. The paper is intriguing and the large bow defines the space beautifully. We selected the color of the ribbon for the dominating oversized bow from the bright multicolored paper. We recommend that you keep on hand a supply of red ribbons in a variety of textures and widths—they are always useful. This tumbling, loopy bow reiterates the many flower shapes in the paper. And the translucent ribbon creates shadows that echo the color variations in the flowers. Here is a festive wrap suitable for any season of the year.

The satin edges of this lovely yellow organdy ribbon, below, help support the extra weight of the multi-looped bow. The white fabric daisy placed at the center of the bow is one segment of a white daisy ribbon snipped off and glued in place. The paper is busy with many colors against a black background. We picked the yellow ribbon to enhance the palette of the paper. The contrasting yellow against black sparkles, while the rounded shapes of the bow loops parallel the petal shapes of some of the flowers on the paper.

B lack and white work with any color. The combination seen here of a delicately wired small gingham black-and-white pattern in a wide ribbon paired with a larger black-and-white gingham pattern in a narrower ribbon dresses up a box wrapped with bright, golden yellow tissue paper. Three glass cherries with barely visible beaded stems and leaves tucked into the bow playfully complete the decoration. The asymmetrically arranged embellishments add a carefree style and dimension to a summertime package.

pinestreet papery

45

ichly colored or subdued, textured, patterned, or solid, ribbons add style to a package. Wired ribbons have become superstars; they are hard to resist. Bows made with these ribbons hold their shape and drape, and can be quickly refreshed. This stunning paper with rows of squares made of four small silver squares on a charcoal gray background is eye-catching. The round, full loops, and the long, draped tails of the orange silk ribbon offer sumptuous texture against the classic, rather formal pattern of the paper. All of this goes to prove that opposites attract.

pinestreet papery

[Above] Think about it—box or no box, bright and colorful or quiet and plain, complementary colors or contrasting, oversized elements or understated, thin ribbons or wide, bow or knot, additional embellishments or none at all. The decisions are many. Tiny folds across the width of this sturdy paper rolled around a cylindrical shape add dimension and texture. Dainty red-tipped white wired ribbons tied in delicate double bows embellish each end of the intriguing package.

The utterly feminine Victorian-style embroidered ribbon that accessorizes the package opposite reminded me of my grandmother, who was always beautifully dressed. I couldn't resist "dressing" the blind-embossed black-paper-wrapped box, complete with pearl necklace tucked at the "throat" to complement the strong, undulating string of embroidered silver dots tracing the ribbon pattern. The package offers more of a décolleté than my grandmother ever would, but this is not a literal translation! The palette is refined, as refined as she was: black, white, and the sheerest mauve organdy. The gift tag, in a coordinated palette, mimics the pearls. You can add style to a project with whimsy and elegance at the same time. And have fun doing it!

The mottled red paper with a gold-flocked floral pattern offers strong graphic appeal. A simple gold satin ribbon tied in a traditional crossed pattern with a single bow is embellished with a charming

Tag: Susan Swan

Christmas tree ornament—a tiny gold mesh-wrapped ball— adding to the excitement of the holiday season. I often add small tree ornaments to our Christmas packages. A playful gift tag, cut to an arrow shape, is topped with decorative papers made by Susan Swan. A ribbon still life, opposite, features a glorious array of gold, red, and black-and-white ribbons.

SPECIAL ADORNMENTS

ven the simplest occasion can become a special celebration with imaginative, decorative wrapping. Special adornments beautifully accent a simple or extravagant package. The adornments can be something special to the recipient, a reminder of the giver, or just something pretty that fits perfectly. Experiment with various sizes, shapes, and colors of materials. Sometimes we need no more than the glorious papers that are their own adornments. The handsome embroidered paper, opposite at rear, is completed by a deep green silk ribbon tied in a classic multiloop bow. The wide ribbon is wrapped once around the package (the short way) and tied off-center for a distinctive asymmetrical design. The pink-and-silver fabric flower ornament on the package at front nestles perfectly inside the featured flocked-dot circle of the pink paper pattern.

pinestreet papery

The whole package at left is a special adornment!
Who could resist this whimsical gift-wrapped
present from pinestreet papery in Sausalito,
California? This is definitely one gift you won't want to open—
you wouldn't want to spoil the wrapping. An infectious sense of
humor permeates the gift. You can't look at the package without smiling or even laughing out loud. A large ball, the gift, is
swathed in white crepe paper and bedecked with Mrs. Grossman's Paper Company's vellum stickers, creating a face, even a
cupid mouth, with stickers. The head is finished with fringed
white hair and a giant sturdy cardboard party hat rolled at an
angle, also bedecked with Mrs. Grossman's vellum stickers. A
yellow ribbon ties the hat on the head, which rests on its own
decorated and fringed stand. A thoroughly engaging gift for all
ages. Bring this gift to a birthday party, place it on the table,
and see what happens.

$S$ometimes you might want to coordinate the design of several packages if you are bringing them to the same place. The square shape of these boxes lends itself to several design treatments—vertical or horizontal, centered or off-center, all with a simple palette.

The packages on these two pages are wrapped with a lovely violet paper, flocked with white. The simple paper is a stunning platform for the natural plant, hens and chickens, above, as well as the two variations, opposite. The wavy purple, grosgrain ribbon supports violet and white flowers created with fabric flowers, and the purple-and-violet-striped wired ribbon ties into a handsome twisted-loop bow.

an paper stamped with giant white hearts, below, offers a big-hearted message of affection. A red bow infuses energy, and the small doll ornament is an extra Christmas gift for a deserving little girl. I love to add special ornaments like these to our Christmas tree each year.

Mrs. Grossman's Paper
Company. Photo: Steve Aja

[Opposite] The paper is straightforward and to the point, the palette strong, the red ribbon a festive note, and the ornaments beguiling.

[Above] A collection of gifts, each decorated with Christmas stickers from Mrs. Grossman's Paper Company, offers a wonderful range of possibilities. The palettes are pleasing, the designs joyous, and the anticipation high.

A little red crab sitting on a black-and-silver pad, as below, is the perfect ornament for a July birthday gift. The silver paper makes an elegant statement together with the rich red-and-black woven ribbon. We wrapped the ribbon once around the box vertically a few inches in from the right side of the box. A second piece of ribbon crosses the first at an angle, creating a sense of motion. The ornament sits where the ribbons cross. It's a good idea to gather unusual trimmings as you see them in shops, online, or at estate sales.

[Above] This sumptuous paper with stunning gold-outlined red flowers on a black background is itself a celebration. A small gold Christmas tree ornament with painted red flowers is the finishing touch attached to a holiday bow of deep red-and-green organdy ribbon with wired edges.

Janet Williams

*D*ozens and dozens of tiny, quilled pink, mauve, and yellow roses scattered over leaves punched from light and medium green cardstock, complete with hand-drawn veins in the leaves, cover the dome of the stunning package on the page opposite. This remarkable project shows the length to which some crafters will go to create the perfectly wrapped gift for a loved one. The quilled roses and punched leaves are glued onto a styrofoam dome (half of a globe shape), which is mounted on a pleated pink ribbon mat atop the soft-green-wrapped box. The scale of the dome on the box is just right. The smaller package at right is decorated with crimped, quilled oversized flowers and leaves. The palette is pleasing, and the crimping folds echo the stripes of the wrapping paper.

Janet Williams

65

mbellishments or adornments add color, weight, and texture to a package. Don't hesitate to add a little extra style—or spice—to your gift wrapping. Let someone know how much you think of them. Gather package embellishments when you have the chance and save them for when you need the perfect finishing touch for a special gift. The gift is multiplied and the anticipation builds even more when an extra gift is on the *outside* of a package. The unusually handsome painted and lacquered wood bird in a tidy bundle of raffia, at left, will sit on a shelf and remind the recipient of a special day.

pinestreet papery

66

*M*an's best friend deserves a present just as pleasingly wrapped as our own. The gift below is one he or she can nibble on while unwrapping. (Dogs love to unwrap presents!) The charming paw print ribbon tied in three vertical and three horizontal rows holds small dog treats at intersections of the ribbons in a diagonal pattern. The symmetrical design, the clean, natural palette, and the edible treats create a delectable delight for a canine friend. Gift time takes on even more meaning when *every* member of the household is included.

pinestreet papery

67

ramatic, imaginative wrapping gives gift giving a whole new dimension—the present becomes difficult to give away. Unexpected additions to a package add a delightful surprise. Earth-colored paper, exquisite garden green wired ribbon, and outrageous faux lettuce and a radish come together at left to adorn an amusingly wrapped hostess gift for an avid cook. Certainly the gift must be something inspired for the recipient's salad-making or vegetable preparation *batterie de cuisine*. It should be fun to track the wanderings of the zany vegetables. On which gift will they appear next?

pinestreet papery

Susan Swan

[Above] Intriguing gift wrap is offered here from an artist who experiments to great effect with shape, texture, and pattern in her paper craft projects. This paper, whimsically called "messy desk" paper, combines coffee cup impressions, ruled papers, and stamps—looking very much like an old blotter from a well-used desk of a fountain pen user. The graphic-style paper is complemented with brown wired ribbon tied in a simple bow and accented with a crafty wooden rubber stamp.

pinestreet papery

limited palette can be very appealing. Contrasting textures and shapes all in white, opposite, create an exquisite design. The peaks and valleys of the accordion-folded ornament extend the play of light and shadow created by the layers of varying shapes, patterns, and textures beneath it. The ornament is created with one piece of white embossed paper wrapping the box. It is accordion-folded into narrow strips, tied with a small piece of wire at the center to hold the pleats, fanned out to form a circle, and attached at

pinestreet papery

each end with double-sided tape. Rectangles, triangles, and one large circle offer geometric play in this refined, elegant gift wrapping. The affection and thought that have gone into the selection and presentation of the gift are seen here at their fullest.

reate a big splash, a moderate wave, or barely a ripple with your gift wrapping. You decide: "Less is more" or "You can never have too much." Choose decorative components with your heart. Gift-wrapping principles are not difficult: choose a color scheme, create a balanced composition with a focal point, and add embellishments. The whole process is easy and wonderfully creative. Try something unexpected to keep you on your toes—a metal nest with a solitary glass egg, at left, or, opposite, a crowded nest of gentle blue eggs of soap. What a celebration!

pinestreet papery

[Opposite] The elegant package of silky gray blue paper wrapped with rich brown ribbons carries an appealing metal nest on three legs, complete with a dramatically speckled blue egg.

[Above] A handsome dark brown corrugated cylinder is topped with a stunning ombré ribbon which anchors a bird's nest filled with eggs of lovely soap. The sensuous palette and shapes reverberate in the deliciously scented soap.

Rose: Judy Ritchie

[Opposite] Playing with materials is so enjoyable! This extraordinary paper called "waves" is stunning. We wrapped the boxes with the paper as simply as possible and played with the embellishments. A handmade red-ribbon rose is placed off-center for a dramatic accent against the dark blue-and-white paper. A rose is easily made with wired ribbon by pulling the wire on one edge while coiling it into a rose shape, adjusting the shape as you gather the ribbon. The folds of the satin ribbon rose echo the shapes of the waves on the paper.

[Above] A white hydrangea sits on the off-center X-crossed dark blue ribbons. And finally, white ribbon is tied inconspicuously in a classic vertical/horizontal cross, embellished with strings of tiny pearl and silver balls. The palette for all three packages is simple, the design classic, and the adornments refined.

pinestreet papery

The zany, long-stemmed flower adornment, at left, reaches sky high, just like the restless classmate years ago who always had a hand waving, begging to answer every question the teacher asked. This cheerful package will bring a smile to anyone's face. The bold, colorful paper supports a nest of ribbon fronds, cut with swallow-tail ends, anchored at the center. They hide the base of the felt flower. Texture can be everything. The deeply embossed yellow paper at right creates great shadows, while a bee sits momentarily on a patch of polka-dot paper deciding his next move.

# FRESH FLOWERS

ike many people, I love flowers. I love them in the garden, in the house, in pots on the deck, in all seasons, in any kind of container, in all sizes of arrangements from one to a hundred blooms, anywhere. A heady scent, glorious color, and a sense of the natural world bring great joy into our lives. As a gift, flowers are sumptuous, and when the flowers themselves are part of the gift wrapping something extraordinary happens: it makes you feel connected to the earth. You don't really need much more than the flowers, the container, and a bit of paper, although it is always fun to experiment. We wrapped and decorated the container for the stunning arrangement of flowers, opposite, very simply. The recipient can remove the wrapping and welcoming fan ornament before placing the arrangement on a table or in a cachepot, but it isn't necessary.

Flowers: Jackquelin Cutrone

Gemma -
Congratulations!

A decorative floral touch can be just that—a touch—or the main attraction. A single flower, at left, captures our hearts, adding vibrant interest to an otherwise simple package. The lush dark green velvet ribbon wrapped around the soft, violet mulberry paper presents the royal purple flower as the focal point of the design. At right, a luxurious bouquet of peonies wrapped with a massive white organdy wired ribbon is featured on an appealing burgundy-colored paper.

Jackquelin Cutrone

83

One of the pleasures of incorporating fresh flowers into the wrapping of a gift is the opportunity to connect with the natural world, with lavish gifts from the earth. How many times have you seen someone lift a bloom from the package to place it in a vase or tuck it in a lapel? Or even to dry the flower and squirrel it away to remember this particular day or moment? The arrangement of flowers on a package need not be anything more elaborate than tucking a few sprigs into the ribbon, knowing that the recipient will save and treasure the blossoms. The cheerful, summery palette of the informal wrapping at left contrasts with the more formal, wintery look of the package opposite. An amazingly different look can start from papers with similar color value.

[Opposite] A small bouquet of soft blossoms is tucked under a bow of saucy orange wired ribbon. The texture and weight of the ribbon contrast with the gentle tones and delicacy of the fragile blooms. [Above] A subtle, calm palette, old-fashioned, formal-looking paper, wide satin ribbon, and delicate lilies of the valley all add up to the recollection of a gentler time and place.

[Opposite] Unexpected treats delight. A small box with its top removed is wrapped with cheerful, patterned paper offering a charming, unusual package of just a few fresh flowers. A thoughtful way to bring sunshine into someone's day! We tucked a block of water-soaked floral foam wrapped in plastic wrap inside the wrapped box. The gift can sit for a while as it is.

[Above] Exquisite floral-embroidered paper offers a perfect setting for a simple ribbon and grouping of three fresh yellow carnations.

Jamie Kilmartin

# Gift Bags, Boxes, and Baskets

*P*aper is not always necessary to create an extra-ordinary gift package. Often, though, and lucky for us, a sense of humor is the *real* necessity. Imaginative, humorous packages are decidedly memorable. A sleek Bento Box (a Japanese lunch box), opposite, offers the ideal platform for a watchful, rather large, faux fish. A strong red-and-black striped ribbon anchors the fish to his perch. Color has much to do with how a designed package is perceived: the red is active and eye-catching, the black elegant and powerful. The two colors together are a difficult combination to beat. And the textures play with the light: a glossy and matte checkered pattern on the box is balanced by the scales on the fish. This package was designed for a man who loves to fish. The handsome box is a keeper, and I bet the fish winds up on a trophy shelf. This lucky man did, after all, catch this fish!

pinestreet papery

Quilled ribbon: Janet Williams

Susan Swan

[Above, left] Why not gather a few flowers, wrap them spontaneously, and bring them to a friend, just because? Here the cut peony and rose stems are wrapped in wet paper towels and then plastic wrap, and inserted into a small paper shopping bag. The striped organdy ribbon, festooned with tiny layered, punched, and quilled flowers glued in place, is tied onto the bag handle. The quiller, Janet Williams, says that when she quills flowers for a project she makes extras to keep on hand to embellish just such spur-of-the-moment gifts.

[Above, right] A small bag made with Abaca pulp netting is a perfect way to present a gift certificate, photographs, or a small scarf or handkerchief. The ocher-colored bag in front is made with watercolor-washed paper, layered first with a panel of gilded paper ribbon and then with a dried-flower-embedded band of Paper Perfect, a paint with actual paper fibers that creates the look of handmade paper.

Judy Ritchie

[Above, left] Charming red, green, and silver small paper bags are decorated with Christmas stickers from Mrs. Grossman's Paper Company and tied with cheerful seasonal ribbons. A ribbon is run through one hole at the top of each bag and out a second hole before tying a soft classic bow with long tails. These small bags are wonderful quick wraps for children's party bags, holiday treats for all, or a small tree ornament for each participant in a Christmas-tree-decorating party.

[Above, right] A small gold bag with a bumblebee organdy ribbon jauntily tied at the top, and a bee-stamped gift tag is a fitting container for a gift of flower seeds for a gardening friend. The larger silver bag at the back, with Mrs. Grossman's birthday candle stickers designed by Sandi Genovese, is ready for any small birthday gift or special treat.

Unique gift wrapping materials are waiting to be found. And sometimes you will find a wonderful gift-wrapping solution where you don't expect it. Why is it that we often have to tell ourselves, or be told, when to stop when we are creating something? The box at left has been sitting on a shelf in my office. It didn't need paper, just a strong-looking, contrasting ribbon and a few faux cherries as imaginative accessories.

Jane Gibbons

pinestreet papery

[Opposite] The dark narrow ribbon against the colorful, narrower stripes of the box creates strong graphic interest. The cherries reflect some of the colors in the stripes.

[Above, left] A gift of a marvelous Japanese green tea came in this silver tin. The tea is long gone and the tin now carries a small gift to a child. The cheery red-and-white diagonal stripe of the ribbon and the teddy bear Christmas tree ornament say that this gift may be opened on Christmas Eve.

[Above, right] A silver metal lunch box is decorated with Mrs. Grossman's vellum stickers and a giant blue bow. No chance of losing this stylishly wrapped carrier in the cafeteria.

ive your imagination free reign and see where it takes you. What could be more fun than packing an individual lunch in an unusual take-out carton complete with a faux lobster tail artfully arranged and attached with a charming black ruffle-edged ribbon? I don't

pinestreet papery

know anyone who would be shy about opening this lunch package. I seriously doubt that we'd find a peanut butter-and-jelly sandwich inside. But then, such a surprise would surely bring smiles all around. The flamboyant white chicken with long, black-tipped feathers, opposite, sits transfixed on a woven black basket tied with a giant black-and-white gingham ribbon. Definitely no ordinary chicken.

pinestreet papery

97

GIFT TAGS
AND CARDS

gift tag on a package isn't always necessary, but when one is included it should be exceptional. Because tags are small, they are easier to make than a 12-inch by 12-inch scrapbook page, or even a 4-inch by 6-inch card. Creating gift tags offers a fine opportunity to improvise with materials and styles. Soft, feminine, and Old World are all terms one might use to describe the charming wrapping and gift tag, opposite. If you could package good cheer, this would be the way to do it, the way to keep a bit of summer in your days all year long. Watercolors add a slightly irregular washed pattern to the paper, which is then sprayed with white webbing to create texture. The tag is an engaging collage on cardstock sprayed with webbing and rimmed with gold. Dried flowers and type are embedded in a Paper Perfect paint platform at center. Small dots and fibers complete the tag.

$S$electing materials for gift wrap and tags is certainly satisfying. But, with a little imagination, creating your own paper or tag designs can be exhilarating. It allows you to refine your sense of design while discovering practical ways to implement the ideas. *You* change the shape, color, and composition as you create. It's an inspiring feeling.

Susan Swan

[Opposite] Hand-painted paper that has been scanned and color-adjusted in Adobe Photoshop has a quiet elegance. The tag has a decorative edge adding playful interest.

[Above] Thick, richly textured paper supports a brilliant woven ribbon. The ribbon is interesting enough to use in one vertical straight line. A light-hearted layered tag adds both whimsy and refinement.

103

and-painted papers with coordinated palettes, textures, and themes make intriguing personal statements. Susan Swan, the artist of the project below, experiments with textures and color to great effect.

Susan Swan

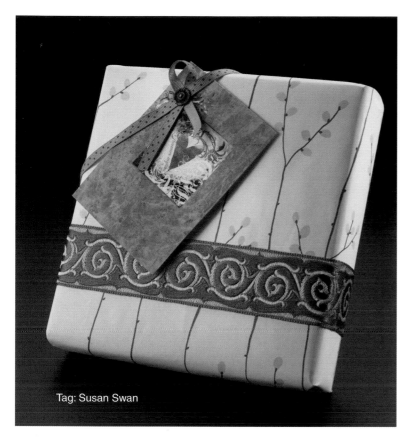

Tag: Susan Swan

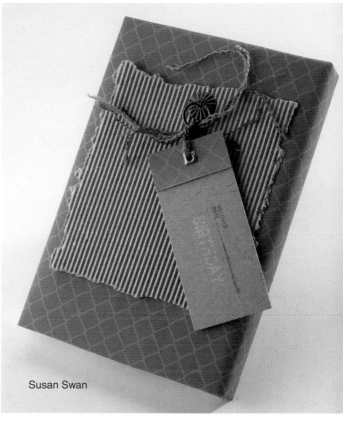

Susan Swan

[Opposite] A modulated palette with an interesting twist results in a striking, creative project. The paper on the top of the box started out the same as the paper on the bottom. The artist created a quiltlike pattern in Adobe Photoshop by weaving lengths of cut orange paper across the paper pattern.

[Above, left] Simple paper, and an extraordinary thick, sculptural ribbon in glorious soft rose and cream colors presented in one powerful horizontal stripe set the stage for an exquisite gift tag extending the palette and adding dimension. This project is all about texture.

[Above, right] More texture and a simple palette. The hand-painted pink and tan paper with a subtle chain link fencelike pattern supports a tan corrugated panel with a torn edge and a gift tag in a coordinated palette. The colors, textures, and fibers all contribute to a sophisticated whole.

Susan Swan

A long, lean, busy package with lots of dots is seen below. Some dots are larger than others, adding a playful note. The heady large dots on the slightly distressed paper are complemented by the small dots on the gift tag. The bright dotted ribbon in a slight color shift serves as a wonderful embellishment. The strong design, opposite, is created with generously sized geometric shapes in primary colors. A slightly smaller blue panel rests on the red package. The blue panel is layered with a striped ribbon on the diagonal and a yellow envelope with strong diagonal lines, inside of which is a red card decorated with a circle embellishment. Strong geometric shapes in strong basic colors make a strong design.

Susan Swan

and-sponged orange paper on the package opposite, at rear, supports a wide, handmade ribbon strip and a gift tag made with letterforms cut from papers painted by the artist. Color is a powerful component. Notice the effect of the same cut-paper letters on the dark and light tags on the light and dark papers. The red package, front, with a dark green bow focuses our attention on the light cut-paper gift tag. Our eye is drawn as much to the layered ribbons as to the moss green tag on the softer orange package. Experiment with your own papers and embellishments. And trust your own eye about what does or does not work. The color wheel (the rainbow arranged in a circle) is a useful tool that can help you choose harmonious colors, but what's most important is that you choose colors that *you* like, that work together in a way that is pleasing to *you*.

Susan Swan

Susan Swan

Susan Swan

Tag: Susan Swan

[Opposite] A strong graphic design created with wood type stamped and scanned into Adobe Photoshop is the basis for this imaginative, subtle-colored project. The digital file is adapted to create an area to rubber stamp the name on the tag. The tag is printed on cardstock and accordion-folded for an almost sculptural dimension.

[Above, left] You needn't conceal the whole package to create a well-wrapped gift. A shawl or cloak of wrapping can transform an ordinary package into something quite extraordinary.

[Above, right] A black-and-gold-checkered paper sets the stage for a gift tag with black-and-gold- and red-and-gold-checkered embellishments. The red-and-black ribbon connects the two components.

Susan Swan

Susan Swan

[Above, left] A hand-painted block print paper consisting of repeated checkerboard squares alternated with a painted poppies panel is used for both paper and tag. The yellow is homespun and cozy.

[Above, right] Warm hand-painted orange sponged paper is a rich setting for a hand-painted red tag emblazoned with "Good Luck." A ribbon inserted into an eyelet at the top center of the tag is anchored with a heart-shaped brad on layered ribbons at the top of the wrapped box. The palette is warm and celebratory for the good wishes extended to the recipient.

[Opposite] Lovely red paper spattered with streaks of yellow, pink, white, and blue paint is a fitting background for a dramatically layered gift tag dominating the center.

Susan Swan

# HOW-TO BASICS

**Wrapping a Separate Box Top and Bottom**

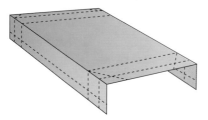

Lay the wrapping paper over the top of the box top to measure and mark the folds. For a careful measurement, place the paper right side down and mark the reverse side. Turn the paper right side up, place on the box top, align the marks with the edges of the box top, and wrap the box.

Fold the paper around the edges of the box top and secure inside the lip with double-sided tape or glue.

Measure and mark the folds for the box bottom.

The wrapped box top and bottom.

## Wrapping a Deep Box

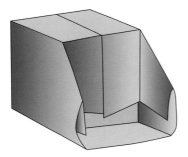 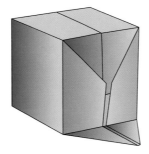 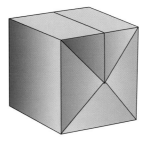

Cut the wrapping paper so that it overlaps about an inch at the bottom (shown at top here) and the ends are a bit shorter than the box height. Place the box face down on the wrong side of the paper and wrap the box, securing with double-sided tape. Fold the top flap down firmly.

Fold in the two sides of the box side panel tightly and secure with double-sided tape.

Fold up the last flap and secure with double-sided tape tucked under the flap. Complete the opposite side.

## Wrapping a Shallow Box

Cut the wrapping paper so that it overlaps at the box bottom approximately one inch and the ends are just a bit shorter than the box. Place the box face down on the paper and wrap the box, securing with double-sided tape along the seam. This seam (shown at top here) will be at the underside of the gift.

Fold in the short ends, creasing along the top and bottom edges. Secure with double-sided tape.

Fold down the flap at top (it will be the bottom flap when the package is turned right side up) and fold up the flap at bottom (it will be the top flap when package is turned right side up) at each end and secure with double-sided tape. Turn package right side up so that the seam is at the back of the package.

## Creating a Reverse Pleat

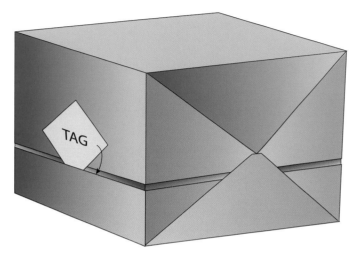

With the paper right side up, fold a pleat in the wrapping paper. Rotate the paper 180 degrees and make a second pleat facing the first one, leaving approximately 1/4 inch space between the meeting folds. Place the gift box face down on the wrong side of the paper and wrap the paper around the box adjusting for the placement of the pleat. The paper seam will be at the back of the wrapped package. Tuck a gift tag in the pleat as part of the package design.

Detail of folded pleat.

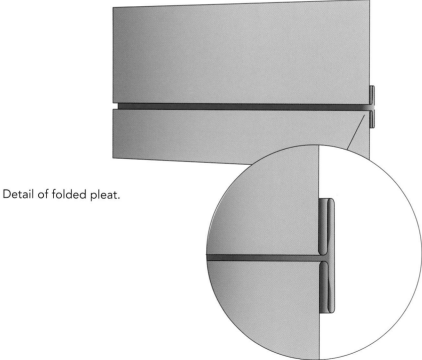

## Tying a Simple Bow

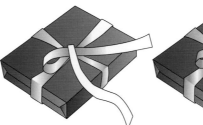

Starting at the front of the box, wrap the ribbon around the box in one direction, crossing at the back to change direction to come around to the front again. Tie a knot at the front. Loop the ribbon that extends from the bottom of the knot.

Wrap the other strand of ribbon down, over, and behind the first loop. Pull it through to create the second loop.

Pull the two loops tight and trim the ends appropriately.

## Tying a Multiloop Bow

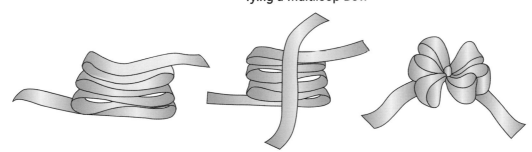

Fold a long strand of ribbon back and forth into a stack of 4 to 6 loops like ribbon candy. Leave long tails at this stage; they can be trimmed later.

Tie a second ribbon around the stack and knot at the back. Slip the knot under the stack.

Twist and fluff the loops, pulling them to an attractive arrangement, and attach to the gift. Trim ends as necessary.

### Creating a Twisted-loop Bow

With ribbon right side up, create a loop overlapping in front. It is best to use wired ribbon for a well-formed bow.

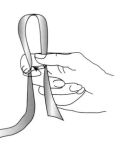

Twist the ribbon at the base of the first loop and hold in place with your thumb. Make a second loop (a figure 8) with that point as the center.

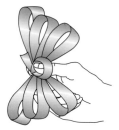

Holding the loops at the center, create 3 to 4 more loops in each direction, twisting the ribbon before making each loop.

Tie a wire around the loops where the thumb holds them and twist firmly to hold them in place. Or tie with a ribbon.

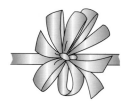

Tug each loop to form a well-balanced arrangement. Attach the multi-loop bow to the package.

Fluff and adjust the loops and bow as necessary on the package.

# SOURCES

**HYMAN HENDLER AND SONS**
21 West 38th Street
New York, NY 10018
212.840.8393
www.hymanhendler.com
Unique and beautiful basic, novelty, and vintage ribbons and trims.

**KATE'S PAPERIE**
1282 3rd Avenue
New York, NY 10021
212.396.3670
    and
125 Greenwich Avenue
Greenwich, CT 06830
203.861.0025
www.katespaperie.com
A chain of stores in NYC and CT with lovely paper, ribbon, stationery, books, and journals.

**M&J TRIMMING**
1008 6th Avenue
New York, NY 10018
212.204.9595
800.965.8746
www.mjtrim.com
Wide variety of beautiful, imported trimmings—ribbons, laces, buttons, and more.

**MAGENTA**
2275 Bombardier
Sainte-Julie, QC J3E 2J9
CANADA
450.922.5253
www.magentastyle.com
Stunning rubber stamps, papers, and embellishments for the paper craft market.

**MRS. GROSSMAN'S PAPER COMPANY**
3810 Cypress Drive
Petaluma, CA 94954
800.429.4549
www.mrsgrossmans.com
The finest stickers, as well as paper and accents.

**PAPER SOURCE**
3333 Bear Street, Suite 125
Costa Mesa, CA 92626
714.957.8555
www.paper-source.com
A chain of stores with fine handmade papers from around the world, plus embellishments.

**PINESTREET PAPERY, INC.**
42½ Caledonia Street
Sausalito, CA 94965
888.660.4050
www.papery.com
Unique, creative, colorful gifts and sumptuous packaging.

**THE GREAT AMERICAN STAMP STORE**
1015 Post Road
Westport, CT 06880
203.221.1229
www.greatamericanstampstore.com
Rubber stamps, ribbons, and embellishments.

**TINSEL TRADING COMPANY**
1 West 37th Street
New York, NY 10018
212.730.1030
www.tinseltrading.com
An amazing collection of unusual and exquisite vintage trims, tassels, ribbons, and more.

# ILLUSTRATED GLOSSARY OF CRAFTING TECHNIQUES

### ACCORDION FOLDING
Accordion folding is a succession of alternating mountain and valley folds across a sheet of paper. See page 71.

### COLLAGE
Collage is a collection of artfully arranged images, papers, or other materials pasted together on a card or object. See page 101.

### CUT-PAPER LETTERS
Paper is an extraordinarily versatile embellishment. Our cut-paper letters consist of painted papers that are cut into small pieces out of which letterforms are created. See page 109.

### PAPER PERFECT PAINT
Paper Perfect is a paint that includes actual paper fibers to create the look of handmade paper. See page 92, right, front.

### PAPER PLEATING
Paper pleating is doubling paper over on itself to form a fold. A reverse pleat is two pleats facing each other on a surface. See page 25.

### QUILLING
Quilling is a simple decorative technique accomplished by rolling thin strips of paper around a slotted tool into various shapes and arranging the shapes to create or embellish a design. See page 64.

### RESIST EMBOSSING
Resist embossing lets you preserve the color of your background paper as part of the design. An area embossed before inking will resist any color applied after the embossing. See page 25, front.

### RIBBON ROSE
A ribbon rose is made by pulling one edge of wired ribbon while coiling it into a rose shape. See page 74.

### RUBBER STAMPING
Rubber stamping is the process of applying ink to a design that has been etched on a rubber stamp bed and pressing the inked image on to cardstock or paper. See page 24.

### STICKERS
Stickers are die-cut images with an adhesive back, allowing them to be easily placed on your cards, packages, or wrapping paper. See page 56.